BUBBLES
The Story of a Little Cat

BY JACQUELINE CHANDLER

ILLUSTRATED BY JANNES NOWAK

Carl Ed. Schünemann KG

Inhalt

This is Cat.

Cat has a black back, a white belly,
    and a black and white face.

He has one white ear and one black ear.

He has three white paws and one black paw.

Cat has no name.

He has no one to look after him.

Cat goes where he likes.

Cat hunts when he likes.

Cat lives how he likes.

Most of the time, Cat is happy.

But something is missing. Cat does not know
what it is. He wants to find out.

Cat sees a bumblebee.

Buzz, buzz.

Maybe the bumblebee knows what
is missing?

The bumblebee flies away.

Cat chases after it.

The bumblebee flies over a field of flowers.

Cat chases after it.

The bumblebee flies through some bushes.

Cat chases after it.

The bumblebee flies over a pond.

Cat chases after it.

Splash!

Cat's paws are wet.

Cat does not like water.

Cat stops chasing the bumblebee.

Next to the pond is a frog.

Ribbit, ribbit.

The frog is sitting on a big rock.

Maybe the frog knows what is missing?

Cat jumps up onto the rock.

The frog jumps into the pond.

Cat does not like water and does not jump
    after the frog.

Then Cat sees a
   little brown mouse.
Squeak, squeak.
Maybe the mouse
   knows what
   is missing?
Cat jumps off the
   rock to ask the
   little brown mouse.
The little brown mouse runs away
   from Cat.
It runs into a garden shed.
Cat chases after it.
The little brown mouse runs behind a
   rake, a hoe, and a shovel that stand up
   against the shed door.
Cat runs behind them too.
Clatter! Bash! Bang!
The rake, the hoe, and the shovel fall
   down, and the shed's door slams shut.

The little brown mouse runs through
a small hole in the shed wall to the
outside.

Cat is too big to fit through the small hole.

Cat tries to find a different way out of
the shed.

He scratches at the door, but the door
will not open.

There are lots of things in the shed.

Can Cat find what is missing here?

Cat looks around.

Cat sees a pile of flowerpots.

Cat wonders if what is missing is under
the pile of flowerpots.

Carefully, he moves the bottom flowerpot
with his paw to have a look.

Crash!

All the flowerpots fall down.

Cat stops looking inside the shed for
the thing that is missing.

Maybe he will find it tomorrow.

Cat settles down to sleep in the little shed.

The next day, a farmer opens the shed door.
Cat runs out of the shed.
The farmer is surprised to see Cat.
Grr!
The farmer is angry when she sees the mess
　　Cat has made, but Cat is already far away.

Cat sees a dog.

The dog's owner throws a Frisbee and
  the dog catches it.

Maybe the dog knows what is missing?

Woof! Woof!

The dog barks at Cat.

Cat runs away.

The dog chases Cat!

Cat runs across a field.
The dog chases after him.
Cat climbs a tall tree.
The dog cannot climb trees.
What a clever cat!

Cat sits down on a tree branch.

He watches the dog below.

The dog is still barking at Cat, but Cat
is safe up in the tree.

Cat settles down and waits for the dog's
owner to take the dog away.

Silly dog.

Cat is high up in the tree.

He can see all around.

Can he see what is missing from up here?

No. He can only see houses and gardens
and trees and monsters.

Monsters are big metal animals
with strange round paws. They have
large shining eyes and make a terrible
noise when they are awake.

Monsters scare Cat when they are awake.

When monsters are awake, they can move
very fast.

For a little cat, monsters can be very
dangerous when they move very fast.

Cat stays away from monsters when
they are awake.

The dog's owner comes and takes the
dog away.
Cat stays in the tree.
Cat watches as day turns to night, and
the lights come on in the street.
At night, the monsters go to sleep.

When a monster sleeps, its shining eyes
go dark, and it is quiet.
When a monster sleeps, its belly is
warm, and Cat can sleep under it.

Cat sees a noisy monster stop at a house.
Soon the monster will go to sleep.

A woodpecker flies to Cat's tree.

Tap! Tap! Tap!

Maybe the woodpecker
   knows what is missing?

Tap! Tap! Tap!

Cat's branch shakes when the woodpecker
   taps the tree.

Tap! Tap! Tap!

Cat clings on to the branch so he will
   not fall off.

Hiss!

Cat hisses at the woodpecker, and the
   woodpecker flies away to another tree.

The wind begins to howl.

Awooo!

The wind blows Cat's fur.

It begins to rain.

Splat!

Large, fat raindrops fall on Cat's head.

Cat looks at the monster below.

Its eyes are dark, and it is quiet.

The monster is asleep now.

The monster's warm belly will keep
  Cat dry.

The monster's big round paw will keep
  the wind away from Cat.

Cat wants to jump down from the tree and
  go to the sleeping monster.

But the tree is very tall.

The tree is too tall to jump down from.

Using his claws, Cat slowly climbs down
the tree all by himself.

What a brave cat!

But one of Cat's paws is sore from the
long climb down the tree and he cannot
walk on it.

Cat limps over to the sleeping monster.
Under the monster, next to its big round
   paw, Cat is warm and dry.
The wind cannot blow his fur here.
Raindrops cannot fall on his head here.
Cat can sleep here.

Cat gives himself a wash.

Cat washes his three white paws.

Cat washes his black ear, and his white ear.

Cat washes his black and white face, his
white belly, and his black back.

Then, Cat carefully washes his sore
black paw.

Now he is clean, and his fur is all soft
again. He feels much better.

But something is still missing.

Cat looked and looked but could not find it.

Maybe he will find it tomorrow.

Cat settles down next to the monster's big
round paw and falls asleep.

It is morning, and the sun is shining.

Cat wakes up.

Rrooaar!

What is that terrible noise?

Where is he?

Then Cat remembers the buzzing bee, the
   splash of the water, the ribbiting frog,
   and the squeaking mouse.
He remembers the clattering and crashing
   in the garden shed and the barking dog.
He remembers the tapping woodpecker,
   his hissing, the howling wind, and the
   raindrops that went splat on his head.
Cat remembers he is under a monster!

The monster starts moving.

Cat needs to run away from the monster.

But his paw is sore.

He cannot move fast enough.

Yoowwl!

The monster's big round paw bumps
   into Cat.

The monster stops moving.

Cat has stopped moving too.

A tall person gets out of the monster's belly
and comes to look at Cat.

Soon more tall people come to look at Cat.

Poor Cat!

Then a small person comes.
Click, clack.

She has four legs like
Cat! But one of
them has a big
white sock on it,
and two of them
are thin and made
of metal.
She puts away the
two metal legs
and sits down next
to Cat.
Now she seems
even smaller.
She is almost the
same size as Cat.
Cat likes it when people are almost
the same size as him.

The small person speaks to Cat.
   Her voice is very gentle.
Oh, you poor pussycat! Are you alright?
The tall people call the small person
   'Angie'.
Cat likes Angie.

The tall people put Cat in a basket and
    put him inside the monster's belly!
Cat has never been inside a monster before.
But then Angie sits next to him.
*We're taking you to someone who will
    make you better.*
As long as Angie with her gentle voice
    is there, maybe being inside a monster's
    belly is not so bad.
Brum, brum.
And the monster's noise is not so terrible
    on the inside.

Angie tells Cat that he has hurt
   his leg.
She tells him that she has hurt her
   leg too.
That is why Angie has two thin metal
   legs now.
The two extra legs help her walk.
Cat is glad he already has four legs
   to help him walk.

The monster stops.

The tall people bring Cat into a white room
  with bright lights.

Humm, humm.

The lights make a humming sound.

There are strange smells that sting
  Cat's nose.

The room makes Cat nervous, but Angie
  is with him.

*Don't be afraid. The doctor will make you
  better.*

The doctor gives Cat a jab.

Meeoow!

Cat falls asleep.

When Cat wakes up, he looks at his leg.
There is a big white sock on it, just like
  Angie's leg!
Cat looks around.
Can he find what is missing here?
No.
But Cat also cannot
  see any legs made
  of thin metal
  for him to use.
Cat is happy
  about that!

Tall people come into the room.
They talk nicely to him, but their voices
   are not as gentle as Angie's voice.
Cat wishes Angie would come back.

The tall people stroke Cat's fur.
Maybe they are trying to give him a wash.
But his fur is dry, so the 'wash' does not
   work properly.

The door opens.

It's Angie!

Cat is very pleased to see her.

Angie also tries to 'wash' Cat, but her hands
   are dry, too.

People are not very good at washing him,
   but it still feels nice.

Cat pushes his head against Angie's hand.

Angie says Cat's leg will get better soon.
Angie says her leg will get better too.
They will get better together!
They will look after each other.
Cat likes this idea very much and tells
    Angie so.
Meow, meow!

Angie says Cat can come and live with her!
Cat likes this idea even more!
Meow, meow, meow!

Angie lives in a red brick house.

In front of the house is a garden with
lots of pretty flowers, and a picket fence
with a gate.

Creeaak.

Angie opens the creaky gate and
brings Cat inside.

The house has lots of rooms.
Can Cat find what is missing in one of
   the rooms?

Cat follows Angie into the kitchen.
Angie puts down a nice big bowl of milk
   for Cat.
Cat is hungry and begins to lap it up.
Cat wants to drink all of the milk … even
   the milk at the very bottom of the bowl.
But to reach the milk he has to put his paws
   on the edge of the bowl.

Cat forgets about the big white sock on
   his paw.
Splish! Splosh!
Cat has upset the bowl!
The bowl turns over and milk spills
   all over the floor.
Never mind, Angie says.
Angie cleans up the milk.

Then she shows Cat a ball of wool.

Angie sits on the floor.

She rolls out the ball of wool.

This time, Cat remembers his big white
   sock.

Cat watches the ball of wool carefully.

The ball of wool rolls in front of Cat.

Whoosh.

Cat pounces on the ball of wool.

Angie tells him what a clever cat he is.

Cat is very proud of himself.

Angie takes Cat upstairs to her bedroom.
The room is filled with toys and books, and
    there is a bed that looks very comfortable.
Angie says Cat can sleep in the bed
    with her.
Cat can smell Angie everywhere in
    this room.
This is now his favourite room in
    the house.

Angie picks Cat up and cuddles him.

I will call you Bubbles.

Cat has never had a name before.
Bubbles … he likes that name.
Bubbles is very happy and proud to have
such a wonderful name.

Bubbles settles down on the warm, soft bed.

Purrr, purrr.

What is that sound?

A purr!

Bubbles is purring!

Angie pets him, and Bubbles purrs even
  louder.

Bubbles likes the sound very much.

It is not the terrible roar or the brum, brum of a monster.

It is not the click, clack of Angie's metal legs or her gentle voice.

It is not the humm of a bright light.

It is not the creak of a gate.

It is not the splish, splosh of spilt milk.

It is not the whoosh of a pounce or even his own meow.

It is a purr.

It is Bubbles's purr.

Bubbles has found his purr.
Nothing is missing anymore.

Wörterverzeichnis nach Seiten

3

this (ðɪs) das
to be (bɪ) sein
cat (kæt) Katze, Kater
to have (hæv) haben
a (ə) ein, eine
black (blæk) schwarz
back (bæk) Rücken
white (waɪt) weiß
belly ('beli) Bauch
and (ænd) und
black and white schwarz-weiß
face (feɪs) Gesicht
he (hiː) er
one (wʌn) ein, eine
ear (ɪə) Ohr
three (θriː) drei
paw (pɔː) Pfote
name (neɪm) Name
no one ('nəʊ wʌn) niemand
to look after (lʊk 'ɑːftə) aufpassen

4/5

to go (gəʊ) gehen
where (weə) wo(hin)
to like (laɪk) mögen, Lust haben
to hunt (hʌnt) jagen
when (wen) wenn
to live (lɪv) leben
how (haʊ) wie
most of the time (məʊst ɒv ðə taɪm)
     meistens
happy ('hæpi) glücklich
but (bʌt) aber
something ('sʌmθɪŋ) etwas
to miss (mɪs) fehlen
to do (duː) tun

not nicht
to know (nəʊ) wissen
what (wɒt) was
it es
to want (wɒnt) wollen
to find out (faɪnd aʊt) herausfinden
to see (siː) sehen
bumblebee ('bʌmbəlbiː) Hummel
buzz, buzz (bʌz bʌz) summ, summ
maybe ('meɪbi) vielleicht
the (ðə) der, die, das
to fly (flaɪ) fliegen
away (ə'weɪ) weg
to chase after (tʃeɪs 'ɑːftə) nachjagen
over ('əʊvə) über
field ('fiːld) Feld
flower ('flaʊə) Blume
through (θruː) durch
some (sʌm) einige
bush (bʊʃ) Busch
pond (pɒnd) Teich
splash (splæʃ) platsch
wet (wet) nass
water ('wɔːtə) Wasser
to stop (stɒp) aufhören

6/7

next to (nekst tuː) neben
frog (frɒg) Frosch
ribbit, ribbit ('rɪbɪt 'rɪbɪt) quak, quak
to sit sitzen
on auf
big (bɪg) groß
rock (rɒk) Stein
to jump (dʒʌmp) springen
up (ʌp) hinauf
onto ('ɒntuː) auf

43

into ('ıntuː) in
then (ðen) dann
little ('lɪtəl) klein
brown (braʊn) braun
mouse (maʊs) Maus
squeak, squeak (skwiːk skwiːk)
  pieps, pieps
off (ɒf) von, herunter
to ask (aːsk) fragen
to run (rʌn) rennen
garden shed ('gaːdən ʃed) Schuppen
behind (bɪ'haɪnd) hinter
rake (reɪk) Rechen
hoe (həʊ) Hacke
shovel ('ʃʌvəl) Schaufel
that (ðæt) welche
to stand up (stænd ʌp) aufrecht stehen
against (ə'genst) gegen
door (dɔː) Tür
too (tuː) auch
clatter, bash, bang ('klætə bæʃ bæŋ)
  polter, peng, knall
to fall down (fɔːl daʊn) umfallen
to slam shut (slæm ʃʌt) zuknallen

8/9

small (smɔːl) klein
hole (həʊl) Loch
wall (wɔːl) Wand
to (tʊ) nach
outside (ˌaʊt'saɪd) außen
too (tuː) zu
to fit passen
to try (traɪ) versuchen
to find (faɪnd) finden

different ('dɪfərənt) anderen, andere,
  anderes
way (weɪ) Weg
out of (aʊt ɒv) hinaus
to scratch (skrætʃ) kratzen
at (æt) an
will do (wɪl duː) tun werden
to open ('əʊpən) öffnen
there are (ðeə aː) es gibt
lots of (lɒts ɒv) viele
thing (θɪŋ) Ding
here (hɪə) hier
to look around (lʊk ə'raʊnd)
  sich umsehen
pile (paɪl) Stapel
flowerpot ('flaʊəpɒt) Blumentopf
to wonder ('wʌndə) sich fragen
if ob
under ('ʌndə) unter
carefully ('keəfəli) vorsichtig
to move (muːv) bewegen
bottom ('bɒtəm) unterste, unterster,
  unterstes
with (wɪð) mit
his sein, seine
to have a look (hæv ə lʊk) nachschauen
crash (kræʃ) peng
all (ɔːl) alle
to fall down (fɔːl daʊn) herunterfallen
to look for (lʊk fɔː) suchen
inside (ˌɪn'saɪd) in
tomorrow (tʊ'mɒrəʊ) morgen
to settle down ('setəl daʊn)
  sich hinlegen
to sleep (sliːp) schlafen

44

10/11

next (nekst) nächster, nächste, nächstes
day (deɪ) Tag
farmer ('fɑːmə) Bauer, Bäuerin
out of (aʊt ɒv) hinaus
surprised (sə'praɪzd) überrascht
angry ('æŋgri) verärgert
she (ʃiː) sie
mess (mes) Durcheinander
to make (meɪk) machen
but (bʌt) aber
already (ɔːl'redi) schon
far (fɑː) weit
dog (dɒg) Hund
owner ('əʊnə) Besitzer, Besitzerin
to throw (θrəʊ) werfen
Frisbee ('frɪzbi) Frisbeescheibe
to catch (kætʃ) fangen
woof (wuːf) wau
to bark (bɑːk) bellen

12/13

across (ə'krɒs) quer über
him (hɪm) ihm, ihn
to climb (klaɪm) hinaufklettern
tall (tɔːl) hoch
tree (triː) Baum
cannot ('kænɒt) kann nicht
clever ('klevə) schlau
to sit down (daʊn) sich hinsetzen
tree branch (triː brɑːnʃ) Ast
to watch (wɒtʃ) beobachten
below (bɪ'ləʊ) unten
still (stɪl) immer noch
safe (seɪf) sicher
up (ʌp) oben

to wait (weɪt) warten
to take away (teɪk ə'weɪ) wegbringen
silly ('sɪli) dumm

14/15

high (haɪ) hoch
can (kæn) kann
all around (ɔːl ə'raʊnd) rundherum
from (frɒm) von
no (nəʊ) nein
only ('əʊnli) nur
house (haʊs) Haus
garden ('gɑːdən) Garten
monster ('mɒnstə) Ungeheuer
metal ('metəl) Metall
animal ('ænɪməl) Tier
strange (streɪndʒ) merkwürdig, komisch
round (raʊnd) rund
large (lɑːdʒ) groß
shining ('ʃaɪnɪŋ) leuchtend
eye (aɪ) Auge
terrible ('terəbəl) schrecklich
noise (nɔɪz) Lärm
awake (ə'weɪk) wach
to scare (skeə) Angst machen
very ('veri) sehr
fast (fɑːst) schnell
for (fɔː) für
dangerous ('deɪndʒərəs) gefährlich
to stay away (steɪ ə'weɪ) sich fernhalten

16/17

to come (kʌm) kommen
to stay (steɪ) bleiben
as (æz) wie
to turn to (tɜːn tʊ) werden

night (naɪt) Nacht
light (laɪt) Licht
to come on (kʌm ɒn) angehen
street (striːt) Straße
to go to sleep (gəʊ tʊ sliːp) schlafen
  gehen
its (ɪts) sein, seine
to go dark (dɑːk) dunkel werden
quiet ('kwaɪət) still
belly ('beli) Bauch
warm (wɔːm) warm
noisy ('nɔɪzi) laut
to stop (stɒp) anhalten
soon (suːn) bald
woodpecker ('wʊd,pekə) Specht
tap, tap, tap (tæp tæp tæp)
  klopf, klopf, klopf
to shake (ʃeɪk) wackeln
to tap klopfen
to cling on to (klɪŋ) sich festhalten an
to fall off (fɔːl ɒf) herunterfallen
hiss (hɪs) fauch
to hiss fauchen
another (ə'nʌðə) einen anderen,
  eine andere, ein anderes

18/19

wind (wɪnd) Wind
to begin (bɪ'gɪn) anfangen
to howl (haʊl) heulen
awooo (ə'wuː) uhhh
to blow (bləʊ) wehen durch
fur (fɜː) Fell
to rain (reɪn) regnen
splat (splæt) platsch

fat (fæt) fett
raindrop ('reɪndrɒp) Regentropfen
to fall (fɔːl) fallen
head (hed) Kopf
to look at (lʊk æt) anschauen
dark (dɑːk) dunkel
to be asleep (bɪ ə'sliːp) schlafen
now (naʊ) jetzt
to keep (kiːp) halten
dry (draɪ) trocken
to keep away (kiːp ə'weɪ) fernhalten
to jump down (dʒʌmp daʊn)
  herunterspringen

20/21

to use (juːz) benutzen
claw (klɔː) Kralle
slowly ('sləʊli) langsam
to climb down (klaɪm daʊn)
  herunterklettern
all by himself (ɔːl baɪ hɪm'self)
  ganz allein
brave (breɪv) mutig
sore (sɔː) wund
long (lɒŋ) lang
climb down (klaɪm daʊn) Abstieg
to walk (wɔːk) gehen
to limp (lɪmp) humpeln

22/23

to give (gɪv) geben
himself (hɪm'self) sich selbst
wash (wɒʃ) Wäsche
to wash (wɒʃ) waschen
clean (kliːn) sauber

46

soft weich
again (ə'gen) wieder
to feel (fiːl) fühlen
much (mʌtʃ) viel
better ('betə) besser
could not (kʊd nɒt) konnte nicht
to fall asleep (fɔːl ə'sliːp) einschlafen

24/25

morning ('mɔːnɪŋ) Morgen
sun (sʌn) Sonne
to shine (ʃaɪn) scheinen
to wake up (weɪk ʌp) aufwachen
rrooaar (rɔː) wrruuumm
to remember (rɪ'membə) sich erinnern
splash (splæʃ) Platschen
of (ɒv) von
to ribbit ('rɪbɪt) quaken
to squeak (skwiːk) piepsen
to clatter ('klætə) poltern
to crash (kræʃ) krachen
to go splat (gəʊ splæt) platschen
to start (stɑːt) anfangen
to need to (niːd tʊ) müssen
enough (ɪ'nʌf) genug
yoowwl (jaʊl) jaauuul
to yowl (jaʊl) jaulen
to bump into (bʌmp 'ɪntu) anrempeln

26/27

tall (tɔːl) groß
person ('pɜːsən) Person
to get out (get aʊt) aussteigen
people ('piːpəl) Leute
poor (pɔː) arm
click, clack (klɪk klæk) klick, klack

four (fɔː) vier
leg (leg) Bein
like (laɪk) wie
them (ðem) sie, ihnen
sock (sɒk) Socke
two (tuː) zwei
thin (θɪn) dünn
to put away (pʊt ə'weɪ) weglegen
to seem (siːm) scheinen
even ('iːvən) noch
almost ('ɔːlməʊst) fast
the same (ðə seɪm) derselbe, dieselbe, dasselbe
size (saɪz) Größe

28/29

to speak (spiːk) sprechen
her (hɜː) ihre
voice (vɔɪs) Stimme
gentle ('dʒentəl) sanft
you (juː) du
pussycat ('pʊsikæt) Miezekätzchen
alright (ɔːl'raɪt) in Ordnung
to call (kɔːl) nennen
to put (pʊt) legen, setzen, stellen
basket ('bɑːskɪt) Korb
never ('nevə) nie
before (bɪ'fɔː) zuvor
to take to (teɪk tʊ) hinbringen
someone ('sʌmwʌn) jemand
to make better (meɪk 'betə) gesund machen
as long as (æz lɒŋ) solange
bad (bæd) schlimm
brum, brum (brʌm brʌm) brumm, brumm

47

30/31

to tell (tel) erzählen
to hurt (hɜːt) verletzen
why (waɪ) warum
extra ('ekstrə) zusätzlich
glad (glæd) froh
to help (help) helfen
to bring (brɪŋ) bringen
room (ruːm) Raum, Zimmer
bright (braɪt) hell
humm, humm (hʌm hʌm) summ, summ
to hum (hʌm) summen
sound (saʊnd) Geräusch
smell (smel) Geruch
to sting (stɪŋ) brennen
nose (nəʊz) Nase
nervous ('nɜːvəs) unruhig
to be afraid (bɪ əˈfreɪd) Angst haben
doctor ('dɒktə) Arzt, Ärztin
jab (dʒæb) Spritze
meeoow (ˌmiːˈaʊ) miaauuu

32/33

any ('eni) keine
about (əˈbaʊt) über
to talk (tɔːk) sprechen
nicely ('naɪsli) nett
to wish (wɪʃ) wünschen
to come back (kʌm bæk)
    zurückkommen
to stroke (strəʊk) streicheln
to work (wɜːk) funktionieren
properly ('prɒpəli) richtig

34/35

pleased (pliːzd) froh
hand (hænd) Hand
good (gʊd) gut
still (stɪl) trotzdem
to feel (fiːl) sich anfühlen
to push (pʊʃ) drücken
to say (seɪ) sagen
to get better (get 'betə) gesund werden
together (təˈgeðə) zusammen
each other (iːtʃ 'ʌðə) gegenseitig
idea (aɪˈdɪə) Gedanke
meow, meow (ˌmiːˈaʊ ˌmiːˈaʊ) miau,
    miau
more (mɔː) mehr

36/37

red (red) rot
brick (brɪk) Ziegelstein
in front of (frʌnt ɒv) vor
pretty ('prɪti) hübsch
picket fence ('pɪkɪt fens) Lattenzaun
gate (geɪt) Tor
creeaak (kriːk) quiiieetsch
to creak (kriːk) quietschen
creaky ('kriːki) quietschend
to follow ('fɒləʊ) folgen
kitchen ('kɪtʃən) Küche
to put down (pʊt daʊn) abstellen
bowl (bəʊl) Schale
milk (mɪlk) Milch
hungry ('hʌŋgri) hungrig
to lap up (læp ʌp) aufschlecken

to drink (drɪŋk) trinken
even ('iːvən) sogar
at the very bottom (æt ðə veri 'bɒtəm)
  ganz unten
to reach (riːtʃ) erreichen
edge (edʒ) Rand
to forget (fə'get) vergessen
splish, splosh (splɪʃ splɒʃ) plitsch,
  platsch
to upset (ʌp'set) umstoßen
to turn over (tɜːn 'əʊvə) umkippen
to spill (spɪl) verschütten
never mind ('nevə maɪnd) Das macht
  nichts!
to clean up (kliːn ʌp) aufwischen

38/39
to show (ʃəʊ) zeigen
ball of wool (bɔːl ɒv wʊl) Wollknäuel
floor (flɔː) Boden
to roll out (rəʊl aʊt) ausrollen
this time (ðɪs taɪm) diesmal
to roll (rəʊl) rollen
whoosh (wʊʃ) husch
to pounce on (paʊns) sich darauf
  stürzen
proud (praʊd) stolz
upstairs (ʌp'steəz) die Treppe hinauf
bedroom ('bedrʊm) Schlafzimmer

filled (fɪld) gefüllt
toys (tɔɪz) Spielzeug
book (bʊk) Buch
bed (bed) Bett
to look (lʊk) aussehen
comfortable ('kʌmftəbəl) bequem
to smell (smel) riechen
everywhere ('evriweə) überall
favourite room ('feɪvərɪt ruːm)
  Lieblingszimmer

40/41
to pick up (pɪk ʌp) hochheben
to cuddle ('kʌdəl) schmusen
such a (sʌtʃ ə) solch einen, solch eine,
  solch ein
Bubbles ('bʌbəlz) Blasen
wonderful ('wʌndəfəl) wunderschön
purrr, purrr (pɜː pɜː) schnurrrr,
  schnurrr
purr (pɜː) Schnurren
to purr (pɜː) schnurren
to pet (pet) streicheln
loud (laʊd) laut

42
roar (rɔː) Gebrüll
pounce (paʊns) Sprung
anymore (ˌeni'mɔː) nicht mehr

Alphabetisches Wörterverzeichnis

A

a (ə) ein, eine
about (ə'baʊt) über
across (ə'krɒs) quer über
again (ə'gen) wieder
against (ə'genst) gegen
all (ɔːl) alle
all around (ɔːl ə'raʊnd) rundherum
all by himself (ɔːl baɪ hɪm'self)
  ganz allein
almost ('ɔːlməʊst) fast
already (ɔːl'redi) schon
alright (ɔːl'raɪt) in Ordnung
and (ænd) und
angry ('æŋgri) verärgert
animal ('ænɪməl) Tier
another (ə'nʌðə) einen anderen,
  eine andere, ein anderes
any ('eni) keine
anymore (ˌeni'mɔː) nicht mehr
as (æz) wie
as long as (æz lɒŋ æz) solange
(to) ask (ɑːsk) fragen
at (æt) an
at the very bottom (æt ðə veri 'bɒtəm)
  ganz unten
awake (ə'weɪk) wach
away (ə'weɪ) weg
awooo (ə'wuː) uhhh

B

back (bæk) Rücken
bad (bæd) schlimm
ball of wool (bɔːl ɒv wʊl) Wollknäuel
(to) bark (bɑːk) bellen
basket ('bɑːskɪt) Korb
(to) be (bɪ) sein
(to) be afraid (bɪ ə'freɪd) Angst haben
(to) be asleep (bɪ ə'sliːp) schlafen
bed (bed) Bett
bedroom ('bedrʊm) Schlafzimmer
before (bɪ'fɔː) zuvor
(to) begin (bɪ'gɪn) anfangen
behind (bɪ'haɪnd) hinter
belly ('beli) Bauch
below (bɪ'ləʊ) unten
better ('betə) besser
big (bɪg) groß
black (blæk) schwarz
black and white schwarz-weiß
(to) blow (bləʊ) wehen durch
book (bʊk) Buch
bottom ('bɒtəm) unterste, unterster,
  unterstes
bowl (bəʊl) Schale
brave (breɪv) mutig
brick (brɪk) Ziegelstein
bright (braɪt) hell
(to) bring (brɪŋ) bringen
brown (braʊn) braun
brum, brum (brʌm brʌm)
  brumm, brumm
Bubbles ('bʌbəlz) Blasen
bumblebee ('bʌmbəlbiː) Hummel
(to) bump into (bʌmp 'ɪntuː) anrempeln
bush (bʊʃ) Busch
but (bʌt) aber
buzz, buzz (bʌz bʌz) summ, summ

C

(to) call (kɔːl) nennen
can (kæn) kann
cannot ('kænɒt) kann nicht
carefully ('keəfəli) vorsichtig

cat (kæt) Katze, Kater
(to) catch (kætʃ) fangen
(to) chase after (tʃeɪs 'ɑːftə) nachjagen
(to) clatter ('klætə) poltern
clatter, bash, bang ('klætə bæʃ bæŋ)
  polter, peng, knall
claw (klɔː) Kralle
clean (kliːn) sauber
(to) clean up (kliːn ʌp) aufwischen
clever ('klevə) schlau
click, clack (klɪk klæk) klick, klack
(to) climb (klaɪm) hinaufklettern
climb down (klaɪm daʊn) Abstieg
(to) climb down (klaɪm daʊn)
  herunterklettern
(to) cling on to (klɪŋ) sich festhalten an
(to) come (kʌm) kommen
(to) come back (kʌm bæk)
  zurückkommen
(to) come on (kʌm ɒn) angehen
comfortable ('kʌmftəbəl) bequem
could not (kʊd nɒt) konnte nicht
(to) crash (kræʃ) krachen
crash (kræʃ) peng
(to) creak (kriːk) quietschen
creaky ('kriːki) quietschend
creeaak (kriːk) quiiieetsch
(to) cuddle ('kʌdəl) schmusen

D

dangerous ('deɪndʒərəs) gefährlich
dark (dɑːk) dunkel
day (deɪ) Tag
different ('dɪfərənt) anderen, andere,
  anderes
(to) do (duː) tun
doctor ('dɒktə) Arzt, Ärztin

dog (dɒg) Hund
door (dɔː) Tür
(to) drink (drɪŋk) trinken
dry (draɪ) trocken

E

each other (iːtʃ 'ʌðə) gegenseitig
ear (ɪə) Ohr
edge (edʒ) Rand
enough (ɪ'nʌf) genug
even ('iːvən) noch, sogar
everywhere ('evriweə) überall
extra ('ekstrə) zusätzlich
eye (aɪ) Auge

F

face (feɪs) Gesicht
(to) fall (fɔːl) fallen
(to) fall asleep (fɔːl ə'sliːp) einschlafen
(to) fall down (fɔːl daʊn)
  herunterfallen, umfallen
(to) fall off (fɔːl ɒf) herunterfallen
far (fɑː) weit
farmer ('fɑːmə) Bauer, Bäuerin
fast (fɑːst) schnell
fat (fæt) fett
favourite room ('feɪvərɪt ruːm)
  Lieblingszimmer
(to) feel (fiːl) fühlen, sich anfühlen
field ('fiːld) Feld
filled (fɪld) gefüllt
(to) find (faɪnd) finden
(to) find out (faɪnd aʊt) herausfinden
(to) fit passen
floor (flɔː) Boden
flower ('flaʊə) Blume
flowerpot ('flaʊəpɒt) Blumentopf

(to) fly (flaɪ) fliegen
(to) follow ('fɒləʊ) folgen
for (fɔ:) für
(to) forget (fə'get) vergessen
four (fɔ:) vier
Frisbee ('frɪzbi) Frisbeescheibe
frog (frɒg) Frosch
from (frɒm) von
fur (fɜ:) Fell

G

garden ('gɑ:dən) Garten
garden shed ('gɑ:dən ʃed) Schuppen
gate (geɪt) Tor
gentle ('dʒentəl) sanft
(to) get better (get 'betə)
    gesund werden
(to) get out (get aʊt) aussteigen
(to) give (gɪv) geben
glad (glæd) froh
(to) go (gəʊ) gehen
(to) go dark (dɑ:k) dunkel werden
(to) go splat (gəʊ splæt) platschen
(to) go to sleep (gəʊ tʊ sli:p)
    schlafen gehen
good (gʊd) gut

H

hand (hænd) Hand
happy ('hæpi) glücklich
(to) have (hæv) haben
(to) have a look (hæv ə lʊk)
    nachschauen
he (hi:) er
head (hed) Kopf

(to) help (help) helfen
her (hɜ:) ihre
here (hɪə) hier
high (haɪ) hoch
him (hɪm) ihm, ihn
himself (hɪm'self) sich selbst
his sein
hiss (hɪs) fauch
(to) hiss (hɪs) fauchen
hoe (həʊ) Hacke
hole (həʊl) Loch
house (haʊs) Haus
how (haʊ) wie
(to) howl (haʊl) heulen
(to) hum (hʌm) summen
humm, humm (hʌm hʌm) summ, summ
hungry ('hʌŋgri) hungrig
(to) hunt (hʌnt) jagen
(to) hurt (hɜ:t) verletzen

I

idea (aɪ'dɪə) Gedanke
if ob
in front of (frʌnt ɒv) vor
inside (ˌɪn'saɪd) in
into ('ɪntu:) in
it es
its sein, seine

J

jab (dʒæb) Spritze
(to) jump (dʒʌmp) springen
(to) jump down (dʒʌmp daʊn)
    herunterspringen

K

(to) keep (ki:p) halten
(to) keep away (ki:p ə'weɪ) fernhalten
kitchen ('kɪtʃən) Küche
(to) know (nəʊ) wissen

L

(to) lap up (læp ʌp) aufschlecken
large (lɑːdʒ) groß
leg (leg) Bein
light (laɪt) Licht
(to) like (laɪk) mögen, Lust haben
like (laɪk) wie
(to) limp (lɪmp) humpeln
little ('lɪtəl) klein
(to) live (lɪv) leben
long (lɒŋ) lang
(to) look (lʊk) aussehen
(to) look after (lʊk 'ɑːftə) aufpassen
(to) look around (lʊk ə'raʊnd)
    sich umsehen
(to) look at (lʊk æt) anschauen
(to) look for (lʊk fɔː) suchen
lots of (lɒts ɒv) viele
loud (laʊd) laut

M

(to) make (meɪk) machen
(to) make better (meɪk 'betə) gesund
    machen
maybe ('meɪbi) vielleicht
meeoow (miː'aʊ) miaauuu
meow, meow (ˌmiː'aʊ ˌmiː'aʊ) miau,
    miau
mess (mes) Durcheinander
metal ('metəl) Metall

milk (mɪlk) Milch
(to) miss (mɪs) fehlen
monster ('mɒnstə) Ungeheuer
more (mɔː) mehr
morning ('mɔːnɪŋ) Morgen
most of the time (məʊst ɒv ðə taɪm)
    meistens
mouse (maʊs) Maus
(to) move (muːv) bewegen
much (mʌtʃ) viel

N

name (neɪm) Name
(to) need to (niːd tʊ) müssen
nervous ('nɜːvəs) unruhig
never ('nevə) nie
never mind ('nevə maɪnd) Das macht
    nichts!
next (nekst) nächster, nächste, nächstes
next to (nekst tuː) neben
nicely ('naɪsli) nett
night (naɪt) Nacht
no (nəʊ) nein
noise (nɔɪz) Lärm
noisy ('nɔɪzi) laut
no one ('nəʊ wʌn) niemand
nose (nəʊz) Nase
not nicht
now (naʊ) jetzt

O

of (ɒv) von
off (ɒf) von, herunter
on auf
one (wʌn) ein, eine
only ('əʊnli) nur

onto ('ɒntuː) auf
(to) open ('əʊpən) öffnen
out of (aʊt ɒv) hinaus
outside (ˌaʊt'saɪd) außen
over ('əʊvə) über
owner ('əʊnə) Besitzer, Besitzerin

P

paw (pɔː) Pfote
people ('piːpəl) Leute
person ('pɜːsən) Person
(to) pet (pet) streicheln
(to) pick up (pɪk ʌp) hochheben
picket fence ('pɪkɪt fens) Lattenzaun
pile (paɪl) Stapel
pleased (pliːzd) froh
pond (pɒnd) Teich
poor (pɔː) arm
pounce (paʊns) Sprung
(to) pounce on (paʊns) sich darauf
  stürzen
pretty ('prɪti) hübsch
properly ('prɒpəli) richtig
proud (praʊd) stolz
purr (pɜː) Schnurren
(to) purr (pɜː) schnurren
purrr, purrr (pɜː pɜː) schnurrrr,
  schnurrr
(to) push (pʊʃ) drücken
pussycat ('pʊsikæt) Miezekätzchen
(to) put (pʊt) legen, setzen, stellen
(to) put away (pʊt ə'weɪ) weglegen
(to) put down (pʊt daʊn) abstellen

Q

quiet ('kwaɪət) still

R

(to) rain (reɪn) regnen
raindrop ('reɪndrɒp) Regentropfen
rake (reɪk) Rechen
(to) reach (riːtʃ) erreichen
red (red) rot
(to) remember (rɪ'membə) sich erinnern
(to) ribbit ('rɪbɪt) quaken
ribbit, ribbit ('rɪbɪt 'rɪbɪt) quak, quak
roar (rɔː) Gebrüll
rock (rɒk) Stein
(to) roll (rəʊl) rollen
(to) roll out (rəʊl aʊt) ausrollen
room (ruːm) Raum, Zimmer
round (raʊnd) rund
rrooaar (rɔː) wrruuumm
(to) run (rʌn) rennen

S

safe (seɪf) sicher
(to) say (seɪ) sagen
(to) scare (skeə) Angst machen
(to) scratch (skrætʃ) kratzen
(to) see (siː) sehen
(to) seem (siːm) scheinen
(to) settle down ('setəl daʊn)
  sich hinlegen
(to) shake (ʃeɪk) wackeln
she (ʃiː) sie
(to) shine (ʃaɪn) scheinen
shining ('ʃaɪnɪŋ) leuchtend
shovel ('ʃʌvəl) Schaufel
to show (ʃəʊ) zeigen
silly ('sɪli) dumm
(to) sit sitzen

(to) sit down (daʊn) sich hinsetzen
size (saɪz) Größe
(to) slam shut (slæm ʃʌt) zuknallen
(to) sleep (sliːp) schlafen
slowly ('sləʊli) langsam
small (smɔːl) klein
smell (smel) Geruch
(to) smell (smel) riechen
sock (sɒk) Socke
soft weich
some (sʌm) einige
someone ('sʌmwʌn) jemand
something ('sʌmθɪŋ) etwas
soon (suːn) bald
sore (sɔː) wund
sound (saʊnd) Geräusch
(to) speak (spiːk) sprechen
(to) spill (spɪl) verschütten
splash (splæʃ) platsch
splash (splæʃ) Platschen
splat (splæt) platsch
splish, splosh (splɪʃ splɒʃ)
   plitsch, platsch
(to) squeak (skwiːk) piepsen
squeak, squeak (skwiːk skwiːk)
   pieps, pieps
(to) stand up (stænd ʌp)
   aufrecht stehen
(to) start (stɑːt) anfangen
(to) stay (steɪ) bleiben
(to) stay away (steɪ ə'weɪ)
   sich fernhalten
still (stɪl) immer noch, trotzdem
(to) sting (stɪŋ) brennen
(to) stop (stɒp) anhalten, aufhören
strange (streɪndʒ) merkwürdig, komisch

street (striːt) Straße
(to) stroke (strəʊk) streicheln
such a (sʌtʃ ə) solch einen, solch eine,
   solch ein
sun (sʌn) Sonne
surprised (sə'praɪzd) überrascht

T

(to) take away (teɪk ə'weɪ) wegbringen
(to) take to (teɪk tʊ) hinbringen
(to) talk (tɔːk) sprechen
tall (tɔːl) groß, hoch
(to) tap (tæp) klopfen
tap, tap, tap (tæp tæp tæp)
   klopf, klopf, klopf
(to) tell (tel) erzählen
terrible ('terəbəl) schrecklich
that (ðæt) welche
the (ðə) der, die, das
the same (ðə seɪm) derselbe, dieselbe,
   dasselbe
them (ðem) sie, ihnen
then (ðen) dann
there are (ðeə ɑː) es gibt
thin (θɪn) dünn
thing (θɪŋ) Ding
this (ðɪs) das
this time (ðɪs taɪm) diesmal
three (θriː) drei
through (θruː) durch
to (tʊ) nach
to throw (θrəʊ) werfen
together (tə'geðə) zusammen
tomorrow (tʊ'mɒrəʊ) morgen
too (tuː) auch, zu
toys (tɔɪz) Spielzeug

tree (tri:) Baum
tree branch (tri: brɑ:nʃ) Ast
(to) try (traɪ) versuchen
(to) turn over (tɜ:n 'əʊvə) umkippen
(to) turn to (tɜ:n tʊ) werden zu
two (tu:) zwei

U

under ('ʌndə) unter
up (ʌp) hinauf, oben
(to) upset (ʌp'set) umstoßen
upstairs (ʌp'steəz) die Treppe hinauf
(to) use (ju:z) benutzen

V

very ('veri) sehr
voice (vɔɪs) Stimme

W

(to) wait (weɪt) warten
(to) wake up (weɪk ʌp) aufwachen
(to) walk (wɔ:k) gehen
wall (wɔ:l) Wand
(to) want (wɒnt) wollen
warm (wɔ:m) warm
wash (wɒʃ) Wäsche

(to) wash (wɒʃ) waschen
(to) watch (wɒtʃ) beobachten
water ('wɔ:tə) Wasser
way (weɪ) Weg
wet (wet) nass
what (wɒt) was
when (wen) wenn
where (weə) wo(hin)
white (waɪt) weiß
whoosh (wʊʃ) husch
why (waɪ) warum
will do (wɪl du:) tun werden
wind (wɪnd) Wind
(to) wish (wɪʃ) wünschen
with (wɪð) mit
(to) wonder ('wʌndə) sich fragen
wonderful ('wʌndəfəl) wunderschön
woodpecker ('wʊdˌpekə) Specht
woof (wu:f) wau
(to) work (wɜ:k) funktionieren

Y

yoowwl (jaʊl) jaauuul
you (ju:) du
(to) yowl (jaʊl) jaulen